ALL-IN-ONE
Rotary Cutting
MAGIC
with **Omnigrid**®

- Handy Reference Tool
- 18 Geometric Shapes
- Problem Solving Guide

C&T PUBLISHING

Nancy Johnson-Srebro

Text copyright © 2007 Silver Star, Inc.

Illustrations copyright © 2007 Silver Star, Inc.

Photography copyright © 2007 C&T Publishing, Inc.

PUBLISHER: Amy Marson

EDITORIAL DIRECTOR: Gailen Runge

ACQUISITIONS EDITOR: Jan Grigsby

EDITOR: Liz Aneloski

TECHNICAL EDITORS: Ellen Pahl and Nanette S. Zeller

COPYEDITOR/PROOFREADER: Wordfirm Inc.

COVER DESIGNER/DESIGN DIRECTOR/BOOK DESIGNER: Kristen Yenche

ILLUSTRATOR: Tim Manibusan

PRODUCTION COORDINATOR: Tim Manibusan

PHOTOGRAPHY: Luke Mulks and Diane Pedersen

Published by C&T Publishing, Inc., P.O. Box 1456, Lafayette, CA 94549

Library of Congress Cataloging-in-Publication Data

Johnson-Srebro, Nancy.
  All-in-one rotary cutting magic with Omnigrid : handy reference tool, 18 geometric shapes, problem solving guide / Nancy Johnson-Srebro.
      p. cm.
  ISBN-13: 978-1-57120-984-9 (paper trade : alk. paper)
  ISBN-10: 1-57120-984-0 (paper trade : alk. paper)
  1. Patchwork. 2. Rotary cutting. I. Title.

TT835.J5857 2007
746.46'041--dc22

                                2006101026

Printed in China

10 9 8 7 6 5 4 3 2 1

Dedication

This book is dedicated to:

Randy and Peggy Schafer. Although Randy passed away in 2003, his foresight and contributions to the quilting industry will live on forever. Peggy has been a steadfast friend since 1990, and she continues to amaze me with her futuristic insights on the evolution of rotary cutting equipment. Together, Randy and Peggy have changed the way quilters make quilts. I sincerely thank them.

My longtime editor, Liz Aneloski. This book would not have been possible without her help. My hat is off to her again for another fine job!

Acknowledgments

Special thanks to:

Prym Consumer USA, the owners of Omnigrid since 1999, for their commitment to maintaining high quality standards for their quilt-making products, as Randy and Peggy Schafer did from the start.

Robert Kaufman Co., Inc. for providing the fabrics used in the book.

C&T Publishing and Teresa Settles of Prym Consumer USA for realizing the importance of updating this book.

Ellen Pahl, my technical editor and friend. I can always count on her.

The thousands of students who have taken my rotary cutting classes.

My husband, Frank. Being his life partner has made me a better person.

Contents

Rotary Cutting Equipment

The year 1988 was a bittersweet one for me. I was suffering with wrist pain, and I had to have wrist operations for carpal tunnel syndrome. After taking a few weeks off to recuperate, I was ready to charge ahead with quiltmaking. To my surprise, I had to re-evaluate how I was rotary cutting and what type of equipment I was using. I had been unknowingly stressing my hands when quiltmaking. Through trial and error, I developed methods that have helped thousands overcome rotary cutting problems. In the following pages, you'll find useful information that will help you rotary cut better than ever.

Basic rotary cutting equipment consists of a trio of tools: rotary cutters, mats, and rulers. I'll explain how to use each one accurately, efficiently, and correctly in the pages that follow.

Omnigrid Rotary Cutter

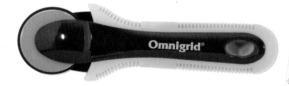

The rotary cutter has proven to be invaluable. This piece of equipment has almost totally replaced those large dressmaking scissors in quiltmaking. The reason for this is accuracy. When you cut with scissors, the fabric is lifted slightly off the table, which makes your cutting inaccurate. This inaccuracy is eliminated when you use a rotary cutter because you are not lifting the fabric off the mat, and because you are cutting against a perfectly straight edge, the ruler.

HOLDING THE ROTARY CUTTER

After surgery on my wrists, I discovered that I had been holding my cutter improperly. Keep the following in mind.

DO Place the bottom of the rotary cutter in the palm of your hand and your first finger on the etched ridge on the side of the cutter; your hand will fall naturally at your side, and the back of your hand will face forward.

DON'T Don't hold the cutter with all your fingers wrapped around the handle. If you hold the cutter this way, the bottom of the cutter will not be in the palm of your hand, and your hand will not fall naturally to your side. Your wrist will be slightly twisted. This position forces your wrist to do all the work while you are cutting. Many people hold their cutter this way.

DON'T Don't hold the cutter with your thumb on top of the cutter and your fingers wrapped around its handle. Your wrist has to work even harder.

I've found that both of the "don't" positions cause pain in the wrist area. Try holding your rotary cutter in each of the three positions. You will notice how much more comfortable the cutter will feel in the palm of your hand when you hold it in the first position; you will also notice the increased control you have when rotary cutting.

FEATURES OF THE 45MM OMNIGRID ROTARY CUTTER

■ The large handle is perfect for most people's hands. The larger diameter of the handle is more comfortable for your hand, especially if you suffer from carpal tunnel syndrome or arthritis. The comfort comes from the diameter of the handle, not the size of the blade.

■ The etched ridge on the side of the cutter is a wonderful feature. This ridge is designed for the placement of your first finger. Placing your first finger on the etched ridge allows you to steer the rotary cutter to keep it next to the ruler.

ROTARY CUTTER IN HAND WITH FIRST FINGER ON ETCHED RIDGE

■ The blade is covered by a pressure-sensitive safety guard. The safety guard slides back when pressure is applied, exposing the blade so that you can cut through the fabric. Once you lift the cutter from the fabric, the guard slides back into place, covering the blade and providing protection. When you're done rotary cutting, push the small lever on the back of the cutter to the "lock" position.

■ The cutter is made for left- and right-handed people. You don't have to switch the blade from one side of the cutter to the other. Since I cut both left- and right-handed, I found this feature to be a plus.

Helpful Hints
for Successful Rotary Cutting

■ If your rotary cutter drags through the fabric, check the following:

You are not holding the cutter at a 45° angle (relative to the cutting mat and ruler). This is a common problem. If you hold the cutter at a lesser angle, you can't apply as much cutting pressure. Also, the fabric may bind against the back of the cutter.

The blade is not butted against the ruler. Do not tilt the cutter toward or away from the ruler.

The tension on the blade is too loose or too tight. Loosen or tighten the screw as appropriate.

The blade is dull. Change the blade.

You need to put more pressure on the cutter when cutting.

You are trying to cut through too many layers of fabric.

■ After you prewash and dry your fabric, you will find that it is much easier to rotary cut and sew if you press it using a sizing product (such as Magic Sizing). This spray sizing (not starch) puts the body back into the fabric.

■ Do not use the rotary cutter on surfaces not designed for it. I have seen students try to cut on wood, plastic, glass, and linoleum. These materials will quickly dull the blade.

■ Save the old blades for cutting your child's school pictures apart and for cutting cardboard, wallpaper, and so on. Old blades work wonderfully for these uses.

- Always keep a sharp blade in the cutter. A dull blade causes unnecessary hand fatigue. A dull blade will also make wider cuts in your mat than a sharp blade.

- Replace a nicked blade immediately. As you cut, a nicked blade will miss threads.

- Take the cutter apart periodically for cleaning and oiling. Placing a small drop of sewing machine oil on the side of the blade facing the guard will help the blade turn more freely.

- Replacing the blade in an Omnigrid cutter is easy. The molded parts fit together only one way, making incorrect reassembly impossible. Just unscrew the thumb nut on the back, lift the front of the cutter off, and replace the blade. It's that simple.

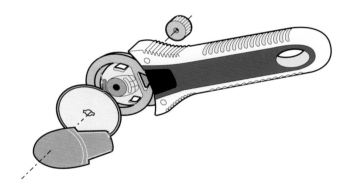

Omnigrid and Omnigrip Rulers

 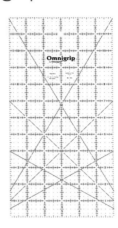

OMNIGRID RULER AND OMNIGRIP RULER

I can say with confidence that Omnigrid and Omnigrip rulers are simply the best. Here are some reasons why I feel this way:

■ Omnigrid manufactures all its rulers for both left- and right-handed people.

The top and bottom of the rulers are marked with two sets of numbers—one for left-handed people and one for right-handed people. I cannot tell you how many times students have told me how happy they are that these rulers are designed for use by everyone.

Left-handed people have told me how hard it is to find products that work for them. To become a better teacher, I taught myself to cut left-handed. So I have personal knowledge of the left-handers' plight.

■ Omnigrid rulers are marked with black and yellow contrasting lines. The yellow lines highlight the black lines, making them easier to see when working with dark fabrics. The black lines are the actual measuring lines. I tell students that when the edge of the fabric is totally hidden under the desired black line, the ruler is placed correctly. If your fabric edge is to the left or right of the yellow line, your cut pieces will be either smaller or larger than desired.

- The lines on Omnigrip rulers are black and green. The green lines highlight the black lines and the edges of the ruler, which makes the lines and edges easy to see no matter what color fabric you are using. And best of all, these rulers are non-slip!

- Both types of rulers have all the markings you will ever need to successfully measure once, and cut once, with confidence. Most of the rulers are marked in $\frac{1}{8}''$ increments, and some of the rulers have the added bonus of $\frac{1}{16}''$ increments (great for miniature work).

- These rulers are laser cut and printed to within 0.002″ accuracy. This accuracy is increased by the fact that the markings are printed on the underside of the ruler, which eliminates the distortion that occurs when you look through the ruler to the fabric.

- If you take care of your rulers, they will last you a lifetime of quiltmaking. All rulers will scratch if you throw them around. Be careful not to place your rulers on top of rotary cutters, ink pens, paper clips, and so on. If you accidentally get glue or ink on a ruler, simply clean the spot with rubbing alcohol. Do not use nail polish remover. It will remove the markings on the ruler.

- Angles, angles, and more angles. These rulers have them all! Once you master cutting straight strips, squares, and rectangles, the next challenge is angles. There are left and right 30°, 45°, and 60° markings on the lower part of the rulers. This placement allows you to work close to your body instead of leaning over your work. These angle markings will allow you to cut diamonds and other shapes faster than you thought possible.

Omnigrid Mats

OMNIGRID MAT; GREEN SIDE   OMNIGRID MAT; GRAY SIDE

I like Omnigrid mats for the following reasons:

- The mats are medium green on one side and light gray on the other. When I started wearing glasses, I found that the bicolored mat was like the gift of sight. By flipping the mat to the side that provided the greatest contrast between my fabric and the mat, I found I experienced less eyestrain. It's like getting two mats for the price of one!

- The grid markings are marked with the same accuracy as the grids on Omnigrid rulers.

- Because the surface of the mats is smooth, my rotary cutter blades stay sharp longer.

- The mats have no odor.

- The mats come in many sizes. You can find any size you need.

- You can safely clean Omnigrid mats. If you happen to get a pencil mark on a mat, you can clean the spot with a tiny amount of diluted dishwashing liquid or liquid cleanser (such as Soft Scrub) on a soft cloth. Rub lightly and then rinse with clean water. For really stubborn stains, I use a small amount of Comet cleanser.

Rotary Cutting

Grain Lines

For accurate shapes, rotary cut strips of fabric on the crosswise grain and then re-cut the strips into the desired shapes.

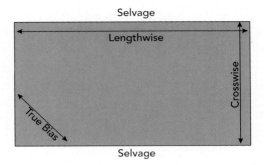

GRAIN LINES

- Lengthwise grain: The threads that run the length of the fabric. There is almost no stretch in the fabric in this direction.

- Crosswise grain: The threads that run across the width of the fabric. There is slight stretch in this direction.

- Bias grain: Bias refers to any diagonal line on the fabric. The true bias of a fabric runs at a 45° angle to the lengthwise and crosswise grains. I refer to a fabric edge cut at any other angle but 45° as an untrue bias edge. Fabric has the most stretch along the true bias.

- Straight grain: Either lengthwise or crosswise grain.

I've worked with fabric for many years, and I have found that few fabrics are woven so that the grain lines (threads) run straight across the fabric. I'm sure the deviations are due to the various processes involved in manufacturing fabric. I try to cut my strips as close to the straight grain (lengthwise or crosswise) as I can.

> **NOTE** To help keep your quilt blocks from getting out of square, try to cut your pieces so that the straight grain (not the bias) is on the outside edges of the blocks or quilt.

GRAIN LINE DIAGRAMS

The following diagrams should help you see where the grain lines are on the shapes. The diagrams will also be invaluable when you are drafting patterns from other sources.

These diagrams are based on cutting strips of fabric on the crosswise grain and then cutting the strips into the desired shapes.

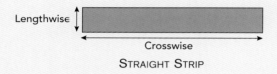

Lengthwise

Crosswise

STRAIGHT STRIP

Lengthwise

Crosswise

SQUARE

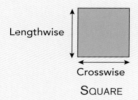

Lengthwise = True bias

Crosswise

HALF-SQUARE TRIANGLE

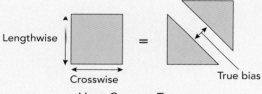

True bias

Lengthwise =

Crosswise

QUARTER-SQUARE TRIANGLE

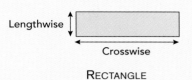

RECTANGLE

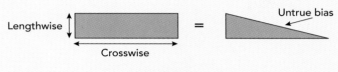

HALF RECTANGLE

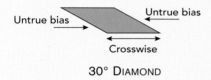

30° DIAMOND

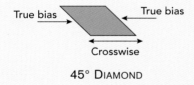

45° DIAMOND

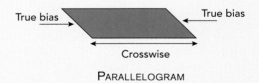

PARALLELOGRAM

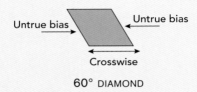

60° DIAMOND

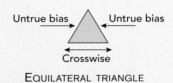

EQUILATERAL TRIANGLE

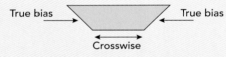

FULL TRAPEZOID (45° ANGLE ONLY)

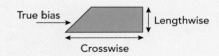

LEFT HALF TRAPEZOID (45° ANGLE ONLY)

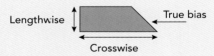

RIGHT HALF TRAPEZOID (45° ANGLE ONLY)

DOUBLE PRISM (45° ANGLE ONLY)

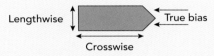

SINGLE PRISM (45° ANGLE ONLY)

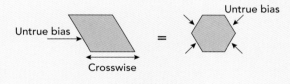

HEXAGON

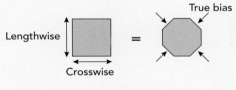

OCTAGON

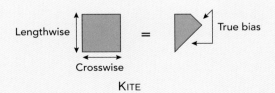

KITE

Squaring Up Your Fabric

To practice cutting a straight edge on your fabric, you will need a 6″ × 24″ ruler, an 18″ × 24″ cutting mat, and a ¾-yard (27″ × 40″) piece of fabric.

1. Fold the fabric in half once, selvage to selvage. The selvage edges of the folded fabric will not be even. Washing, drying, and even the way the fabric was cut at the store can result in unevenness. Make sure there are no wrinkles of fabric along the fold. The fabric will now measure approximately 20″ in width and 27″ in length. Place the fabric on the mat with the fold at the top, farthest away from you. The selvages will be at the bottom, nearest to you.

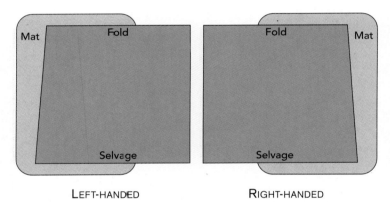

LEFT-HANDED   RIGHT-HANDED

2. Place one of the ruler's short sides (6″) along the fold as accurately as you can. The long (24″) sides of the ruler will be parallel to the left-hand edge of the mat for left-handed quilters and parallel with the right-hand edge of the mat for right-handed quilters.

Firmly place the thumb of your noncutting hand on the ruler over the lower edge of the fabric and your four fingertips 6″–7″ up the ruler. Use your fingertips to stabilize the ruler, not the palm of your hand. Holding the rotary cutter as described on pages 7 and 8, start cutting away from you until the cutter is even with your fingertips.

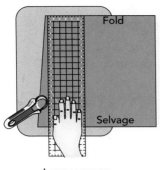

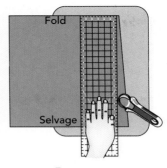

LEFT-HANDED   RIGHT-HANDED

Stop cutting, but don't lift the rotary cutter! While keeping the rotary cutter stationary, carefully move your thumb up to your fingertips. Next, press down with your thumb and move your four fingertips up the ruler approximately 6″. I call this "hand walking." Continue cutting until the cutter is again even with your fingertips. Stop cutting, but keep the rotary blade in the fabric. Move your thumb up to your fingertips. Press down with your thumb. Move your four fingertips up the ruler approximately another 6″. Rotary cut. Continue the hand walking process until your entire strip is completely cut. You have now squared up that edge of the fabric with the folded edge.

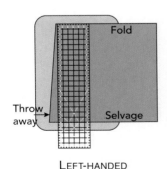

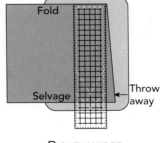

LEFT-HANDED   RIGHT-HANDED

The ruler will not slip if you use the hand walking method.
NOTE   Remember that you want to rotary cut only the fabric that is being stabilized by the pressure of your fingertips on the ruler.

Cutting Straight Strips

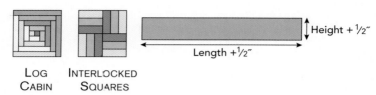

LOG   INTERLOCKED
CABIN   SQUARES

Length +1/2″

Height + 1/2″

Example   Desired finished strip size: $2\frac{1}{2}″ \times 39\frac{1}{2}″$

$2\frac{1}{2}″ + \frac{1}{2}″ = 3″$ $39\frac{1}{2}″ + \frac{1}{2}″ = 40″$

Size of strip to cut: $3″ \times 40″$

To cut long straight strips I always use a $6″ \times 24″$ ruler and an $18″ \times 24″$ mat.

1. Square up one raw edge of your fabric (page 20).

2. Turn the mat 180° (one half turn) so that the fold of the fabric is close to your body. Do not lift the fabric off the mat (lifting the fabric will disturb the freshly cut edge). Place one long edge of the ruler over the freshly cut edge. Move the ruler until the raw edge of the fabric is lined up with the 3″ marking and one short edge of the ruler is even with the fold. Use the hand walking method to rotary cut a $3″ \times 40″$ strip. Be sure to read the next section.

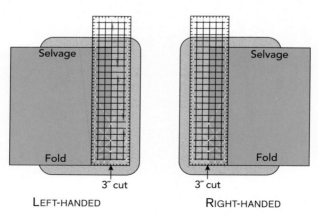

Selvage   Selvage

Fold   Fold

3″ cut   3″ cut

LEFT-HANDED   RIGHT-HANDED

NOTE After cutting one strip, read the next section, Avoiding the Dreaded V Cut.

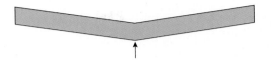

A "V" APPEARS AT THE FOLD OF A STRIP.

To prevent V strips:

- After cutting 6″ worth of strips, you must re-square the fabric with the fold. This process is extremely important to maintain cutting accuracy. After re-squaring, you can continue cutting straight strips until you have cut another 6″ worth of strips; then you must re-square again. Repeat this procedure every 6″.

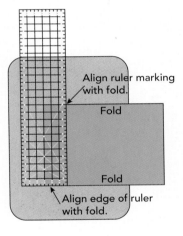

- I fold the fabric only once (two layers) before rotary cutting, but some people like to fold the fabric twice (four layers). Folding twice is not necessarily a problem, but if you are working with two folds, you must align the top of the ruler with one fold and the markings on the ruler with the opposite fold. Aligning the ruler with both folds will ensure that they are parallel to each other.

Align ruler marking with fold.

Fold

Fold

Align edge of ruler with fold.

Remember also that the more layers of fabric you rotary cut through, the more inaccurate your cutting becomes. To prove this, stack six to eight layers of fabric together. Now place the ruler as if you were going to cut a 2″ strip. You will notice that the ruler acts like a teeter-totter. The bottom layers of fabric shift slightly, and this shifting will cause you to cut inaccurately.

Cutting a Square.

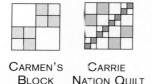

Carmen's Block   Carrie Nation Quilt

Height + ½″
Length + ½″

Example   Desired finished square size: 2½″ × 2½″

2½″ + ½″ = 3″

Size of square to cut: 3″ × 3″

I use a 6″ × 12″, 3″ × 18″, or 6″ × 6″ ruler to recut strips into smaller shapes.

1. Cut a strip 3″ × 40″ (page 22).

2. Place the folded 3″ × 20″ strip on the mat (when folded in half, the 40″ strip measures 20″). You will be cutting through two layers at a time. Place one short side of the ruler along the top of the strip. Square up the short side of the strip by trimming off the selvages, approximately ¼″.

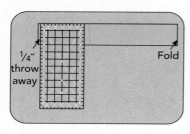

¼″ throw away   Fold

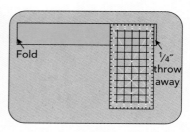

Fold   ¼″ throw away

LEFT-HANDED   RIGHT-HANDED

3. Turn the mat 180° (one half turn). Place the ruler on top of the strip so that the 3″ marking lines up perfectly with the freshly cut edge. Make sure the top edge of the ruler is even with the top edge of the strip. Cut.

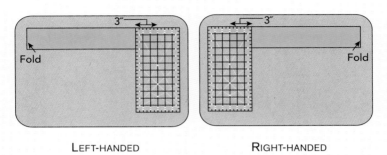

LEFT-HANDED   RIGHT-HANDED

NOTE After cutting 3 squares, square up the edge of the strip again as shown in Step 2 to ensure accurate shapes.

Cutting a Half-Square Triangle

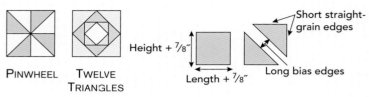

PINWHEEL   TWELVE TRIANGLES

Height + ⅞″

Length + ⅞″

Short straight-grain edges

Long bias edges

> **NOTE** A time-saver for either method is to cut two strips of fabric (a light strip and a dark strip of the desired colors). Place them right sides together, making sure all edges align perfectly, and cut the half-square triangles. The triangles are matched and ready to sew!

METHOD 1

Example: Desired finished short side of triangle: $2\frac{1}{2}″$

$2\frac{1}{2}″ + \frac{7}{8}″ = 3\frac{3}{8}″$

Size of square to cut: $3\frac{3}{8}″ \times 3\frac{3}{8}″$

1. Cut a square $3\frac{3}{8}″ \times 3\frac{3}{8}″$ (page 24).

2. Place the ruler diagonally over the square, exactly from corner to corner. Place your fingers on top of the ruler, directly over the fabric corners, to prevent the fabric from moving during cutting. Cut the square into two triangles.

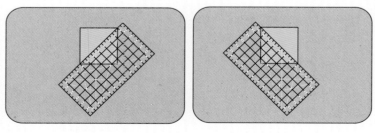

LEFT-HANDED   RIGHT-HANDED

After sewing the two triangles together along the long bias edge and pressing, you will notice that the resulting square has what quilters call "dog ears" at the corners. Oftentimes such squares become distorted during pressing. To prevent this distortion, always cut the dog ears off before you press.

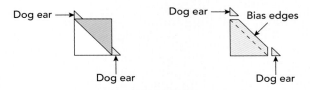

TRIM DOG EARS BEFORE PRESSING.

METHOD 2

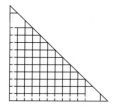

#96 AND #96L HALF-SQUARE RULER BY OMNIGRID

Example: Desired finished short side of triangle: 2½″

$2\frac{1}{2}″ + \frac{1}{2}″ = 3″$

Size of strip to cut: 3″

To determine the height of the strip with the ruler, measure from the dashed line near the top of the ruler to the bottom line of the desired size. No guesswork, the seam allowances are built into the rulers.

The #96 ruler allows you to cut up to 6″ triangles; the #96L allows you to cut up to 8″ triangles.

1. Cut a strip 3″ × 40″ (page 22) and square up the end (page 24).

2. Place the ruler on the strip with the dashed tip of the ruler extending beyond the top of the strip and the 2½″ marking along the bottom of the strip. Cut.

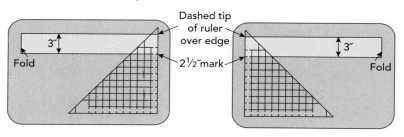

LEFT-HANDED   RIGHT-HANDED

You will notice that triangles cut with this method have only one dog ear. Trim the single dog ear off after sewing the triangles together, but before pressing.

Dog ear

3. Rotate the ruler 180°. Line up the 2½″ marking along the top of the strip; the dashed line will be along the bottom of the strip. The diagonal edge of the ruler will line up with the freshly cut diagonal edge of the fabric. Cut again.

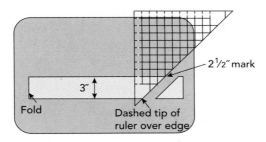

LEFT-HANDED

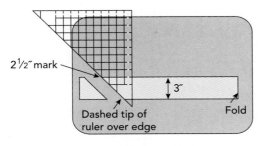

RIGHT-HANDED

4. To cut more triangles, continue rotating the ruler each time. Don't forget to occasionally re-square the short end of the strip.

Cutting a Quarter-Square Triangle

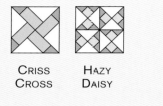

CRISS
CROSS

HAZY
DAISY

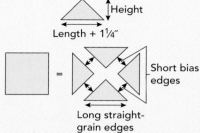

Height

Length + 1¼"

Short bias edges

Long straight-grain edges

METHOD 1

Example: Desired finished length of long side of quarter-square triangle: $3\frac{3}{4}$"

$3\frac{3}{4}" + 1\frac{1}{4}" = 5"$

Size of square to cut: $5" \times 5"$

1. Cut a square $5" \times 5"$ (page 24).

2. Place the ruler diagonally over the square, exactly from corner to corner. Place your fingers on top of the ruler, directly over the fabric corners, to prevent the fabric from moving during cutting. Cut the square into two triangles. Do not separate the two triangles.

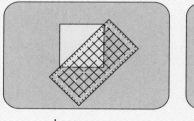
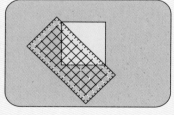

LEFT-HANDED

RIGHT-HANDED

3. Cut the square in half again, placing the ruler on the opposite corners.

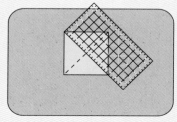
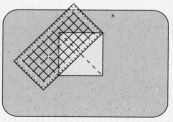

LEFT-HANDED

RIGHT-HANDED

METHOD 2

Length

Height

Short bias edges

Long straight-grain edge

#98 AND #98L QUARTER-
SQUARE RULERS
BY OMNIGRID

The #98 and #98L rulers allow you to cut up to 8″ and 12″ triangles (long side).

> **NOTE** These rulers are great when you need only one or two quarter-square triangles. With Method 1, you would waste the remaining two or three cut triangles. These rulers are also perfect if you want to control the direction of a striped or plaid fabric.

A triangle cut at the 5″ marking of the ruler will finish to be 5″ on the long side. The length of the 5″ marking on the ruler is actually 6¼″ (as in Method 1, finished size + 1¼″). No math is required because the seam allowances are built into the rulers.

Example: Desired finished length of long side of quarter-square triangle: 5″

Size of strip to cut: Measure from the top point of the ruler to the 5″ line = 3⅛″

1. Cut a strip 3⅛″ × 40″ (page 22).

2. Place the ruler on the strip so that the 5″ marking is along the bottom of the strip. The top of the ruler should be touching the top of the strip. Cut along each angled edge of the ruler.

3. Rotate the ruler 180° and place the 5″ marking along the top of the strip. Cut again.

4. Continue rotating the ruler each time to cut more triangles. Be sure to keep an accurate 45° angle while cutting; check the angle and re-cut it to an exact 45° as often as needed.

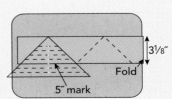

3⅛″

Fold

5″ mark

Cutting a Rectangle

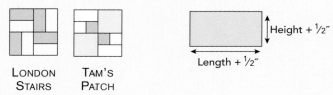

LONDON STAIRS   TAM'S PATCH

Height + $\frac{1}{2}''$

Length + $\frac{1}{2}''$

I call a rectangle that is twice as long as it is high, or vice versa, a true rectangle. For example, 2″ × 4″ and 3″ × 6″ rectangles are true rectangles. An untrue rectangle can be any size. Both types of rectangles are cut in the same way.

Example: Desired finished rectangle size: $2\frac{1}{2}'' \times 5''$

$2\frac{1}{2}'' + \frac{1}{2}'' = 3''$ $5'' + \frac{1}{2}'' = 5\frac{1}{2}''$

Size of rectangle to cut: $3'' \times 5\frac{1}{2}''$

1. Cut a strip 3″ × 40″ (page 22) and square up the end (page 24).

2. Turn the mat 180° (one half turn). Place the ruler on top of the strip so that the $5\frac{1}{2}''$ marking lines up with the newly cut edge. Make sure the top of the ruler is even with the top of the strip. Cut.

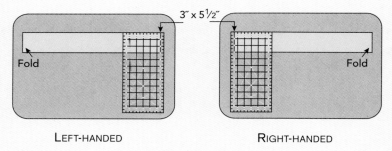

LEFT-HANDED   RIGHT-HANDED

NOTE After cutting three rectangles, re-square the short edge of the strip to ensure accuracy.

Cutting a Half Rectangle

  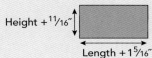

LACY LATTICE MAGNOLIA   TRUE RECTANGLE
WORK   BUD

You can easily cut a true (page 32) or untrue rectangle in half diagonally. You will need to add different dimensions for seam allowances to an untrue rectangle. See the second note below.

Example: Desired finished true rectangle size: $2'' \times 4''$

$$2'' + {}^{11}\!/_{16}'' = 2{}^{11}\!/_{16}'' \qquad 4'' + 1{}^{5}\!/_{16}'' = 5{}^{5}\!/_{16}''$$

Size of rectangle to cut: $2{}^{11}\!/_{16}'' \times 5{}^{5}\!/_{16}''$

1. Cut a rectangle $2{}^{11}\!/_{16}'' \times 5{}^{5}\!/_{16}''$ (page 32). ($2{}^{11}\!/_{16}''$ is between $2{}^{5}\!/_{8}''$ and $2{}^{3}\!/_{4}''$; $5{}^{5}\!/_{16}''$ is between $5{}^{1}\!/_{4}''$ and $5{}^{3}\!/_{8}''$.)

2. Place the ruler diagonally over the rectangle, exactly from corner to corner. Place your fingers on top of the ruler, directly over the fabric corners, to prevent the fabric from moving during cutting. Cut into two half rectangles.

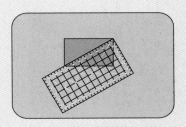 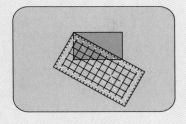

LEFT-HANDED   RIGHT-HANDED

NOTE To make mirror images of this shape, place two rectangles wrong sides together and then rotary cut as shown.

NOTE To determine the add-on seam allowance for an untrue half rectangle, draw the finished size rectangle on paper. Draw a diagonal line from corner to corner. Then draw a $\frac{1}{4}''$ seam allowance around the half rectangle. This will be the cutting measurement for the unfinished size of an untrue half rectangle. Rotary cut as shown.

Cutting a 30° Diamond

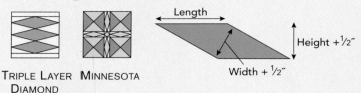

TRIPLE LAYER MINNESOTA
DIAMOND

The height and width must be the same. You do not need to calculate the length; it will be correct after cutting.

Example: Desired finished diamond size: $2\frac{1}{2}''$ height

$$2\frac{1}{2}'' + \frac{1}{2}'' = 3''$$

Height of strip to cut: $3''$

1. Cut a strip $3'' \times 40''$ (page 22).

2. Place the ruler on top of the strip, lining up the 30° marking with the bottom of the strip. Cut.

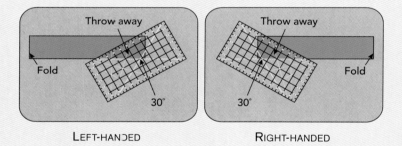

LEFT-HANDED   RIGHT-HANDED

3. Find the 3″ marking on the top or bottom of the ruler. Do not look at the numbers on the edges of the ruler. Place the ruler diagonally on the strip so the 3″ marking is on the freshly cut 30° edge. Also make sure the 30° marking is on the bottom of the strip. Cut. If you fold the diamond in half, long point to long point, all the edges will match.

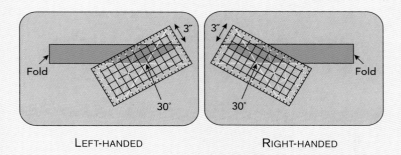

LEFT-HANDED   RIGHT-HANDED

Cutting a 45° Diamond

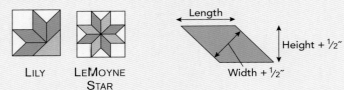

LILY | LEMOYNE STAR

Length

Height + ½″

Width + ½″

The height and width of a 45° diamond MUST be the same. You do not need to calculate the length; it will be correct after cutting.

Example: Desired finished diamond size: 2½″ height

$2\frac{1}{2}″ + \frac{1}{2}″ = 3″$

Height of strip to cut: 3″

1. Cut a strip 3″ × 40″ (page 22).

2. Place the ruler on top of the strip, lining up the 45° line with the bottom of the strip. Cut.

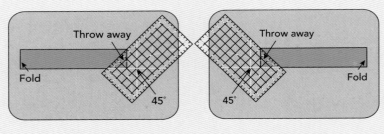

Throw away

Fold

45°

LEFT-HANDED

Throw away

Fold

45°

RIGHT-HANDED

3. Find the 3″ marking on the top or bottom of the ruler. Do not look at the numbers on the edges of the ruler. Place the ruler diagonally on the strip so the 3″ marking is on the freshly cut 45° edge. Also make sure the 45° marking is on the bottom of the strip. Cut. If you fold the diamond in half, long point to long point, everything will match.

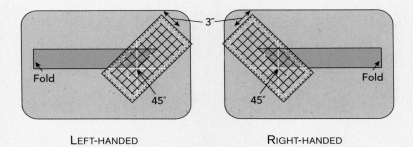

LEFT-HANDED   RIGHT-HANDED

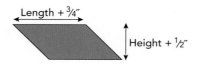

FLOWER
BASKET

RED AND
WHITE CROSS

The width of the diagonal cut will NOT be the same as the height of the strip.

Example: Desired finished parallelogram size: $2\frac{1}{2}'' \times 6\frac{3}{8}''$

$2\frac{1}{2}'' + \frac{1}{2}'' = 3''$ $6\frac{3}{8}'' + \frac{3}{4}'' = 7\frac{1}{8}''$

Height of strip to cut: $3''$

1. Cut a strip $3'' \times 40''$ (page 22).

2. Make a 45° cut (page 36).

3. Measure across the top of the strip $7\frac{1}{8}''$ and place a small pencil mark.

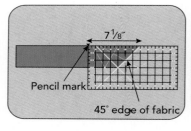

LEFT-HANDED

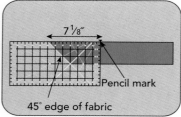

RIGHT-HANDED

4. Place the ruler diagonally on the strip so that the 45° marking is on the bottom of the strip and the edge of the ruler lines up with the pencil mark. The number on the ruler that lines up with the freshly cut 45° edge is the width (5″). Cut. If you fold the parallelogram in half, long point to long point, it will not match. If it does match, you have cut a 45° diamond, not a parallelogram.

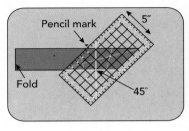

LEFT-HANDED

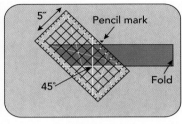

RIGHT-HANDED

Cutting a 60° Diamond

NOVEL
STAR

CUBE
WORK

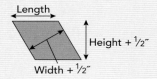

Length

Height + ½″

Width + ½″

The height and width of a 60° diamond must be the same. You do not need to calculate the length; it will be correct after cutting.

Example: Desired finished diamond size: 2½″ height

$2\frac{1}{2}″ + \frac{1}{2}″ = 3″$

Height of strip to cut: 3″

1. Cut a strip 3″ × 40″ (page 22).

2. Place the ruler on top of the strip, lining up the 60° line with the bottom of the strip. Cut.

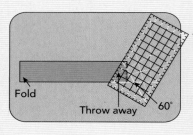

Fold

Throw away   60°

LEFT-HANDED

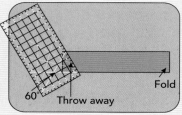

60°   Throw away

Fold

RIGHT-HANDED

3. Find the 3″ marking on the top or bottom of the ruler. Do not look at the numbers on the edges of the ruler. Place the ruler diagonally on the strip so the 3″ marking is on the freshly cut 60° edge. Also make sure the 60° marking is on the bottom of the strip. Cut. If you fold the diamond in half, long point to long point, everything will match.

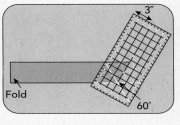

LEFT-HANDED

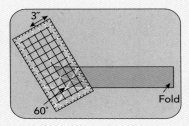

RIGHT-HANDED

Cutting an Equilateral Triangle

  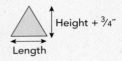

Height + ¾″

Length

SIMPLE TREE   HEXAGON

An equilateral triangle is a triangle with all three sides of equal length. You need to know only the unfinished height of an equilateral triangle in order to cut.

Example: Desired finished height: 2¼″

2¼″ + ¾″ = 3″

Width of strip to cut: 3″

> **NOTE** The length will automatically be correct after you rotary cut the triangle.

1. Cut a strip 3″ × 40″ (page 22).

2. Place the ruler on top of the strip, lining up the 60° marking with the bottom of the strip. Cut.

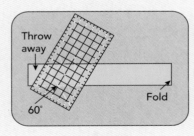

Throw away

Fold

60°

LEFT-HANDED

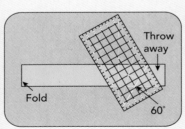

Throw away

Fold

60°

RIGHT-HANDED

3. Rotate the ruler so that the opposite 60° marking is on the bottom of the strip. Carefully slide the ruler until it lines up with the sharp point of the original cut. Cut. To make more triangles, just rotate the ruler between the appropriate 60° markings until you have the desired number of triangles.

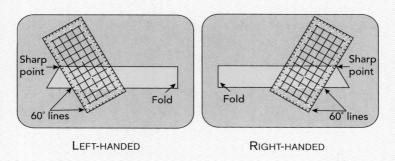

LEFT-HANDED   RIGHT-HANDED

Cutting a Full Trapezoid

LITTLE SHIP
O' DREAMS

SPOOL

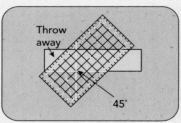

Height + $\frac{1}{2}$″

Length + $1\frac{1}{4}$″

A full trapezoid is actually a rectangle with both ends cut off at an angle. The ends can be cut at the same angle or at different angles. Trapezoids used in quiltmaking usually have ends that are both cut at 45°.

Example: Desired finished trapezoid size: $2\frac{1}{2}$″ × 9″

$2\frac{1}{2}$″ + $\frac{1}{2}$″ = 3″   9″ + $1\frac{1}{4}$″ = $10\frac{1}{4}$″

Size of rectangle to cut: 3″ × $10\frac{1}{4}$″

1. Cut a rectangle 3″ × $10\frac{1}{4}$″ (page 32).

2. Place the ruler so that the 45° marking on the lower edge lines up with the bottom of the rectangle. Carefully slide the ruler so that you will be starting the cut exactly at the lower corner of the rectangle. If you start the cut to the left or right of the exact corner, your trapezoid will not be the correct size. Cut.

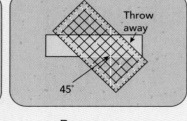

LEFT-HANDED

RIGHT-HANDED

3. Turn the mat 180° (one half turn). Place the ruler so that the opposite 45° marking is aligned with the bottom of the rectangle. Carefully slide the ruler so that you will be finishing the cut exactly at the upper corner of the rectangle. Cut.

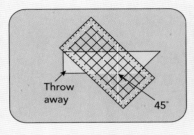

LEFT-HANDED

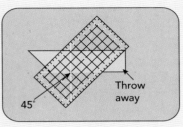

RIGHT-HANDED

Cutting a Half Trapezoid

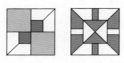

UNNAMED TWIN DARTS

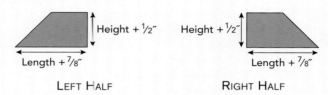

Height + ½″

Length + ⅞″

LEFT HALF

Height + ½″

Length + ⅞″

RIGHT HALF

Half trapezoids used in quiltmaking have one end that is cut at an angle, usually 45°.

Example: Desired finished half trapezoid size: $2\frac{1}{2}$″ × 6″

$2\frac{1}{2}$″ + $\frac{1}{2}$″ = 3″   6″ + $\frac{7}{8}$″ = $6\frac{7}{8}$″

Size of rectangle to cut: 3″ × $6\frac{7}{8}$″

1. Cut a rectangle 3″ × $6\frac{7}{8}$″ (page 32).

2. Place the ruler so that the 45° line on the lower edge lines up with the bottom of the rectangle. Carefully place the ruler so that you will be starting the cut exactly at the lower corner of the rectangle. If you start the cut to the left or right of the exact corner, your half trapezoid will not be the correct size. Cut.

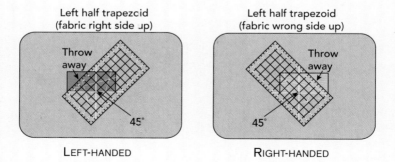

Left half trapezcid
(fabric right side up)

Throw away

45°

LEFT-HANDED

Left half trapezoid
(fabric wrong side up)

Throw away

45°

RIGHT-HANDED

Right half trapezoid
(fabric wrong side up)

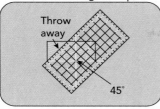

LEFT-HANDED

Right half trapezoid
(fabric right side up)

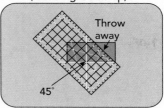

RIGHT-HANDED

TIP If you layer two rectangles, wrong sides together, you can cut left and right half trapezoids at the same time.

Cutting a Double Prism

X BLOCK   PRAIRIE FLOWER

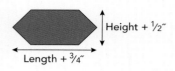

Height + $\frac{1}{2}$"

Length + $\frac{3}{4}$"

You will see how valuable the angles are on the ruler once you cut a single or double prism. In quiltmaking, a single prism is a rectangle with two corners cut off, usually at 45° angles. A double prism is a rectangle with all four corners cut off.

Example   Desired finished prism size: $4\frac{1}{2}$" × $7\frac{3}{4}$"

$4\frac{1}{2}$" + $\frac{1}{2}$" = 5" $7\frac{3}{4}$" + $\frac{3}{4}$" = $8\frac{1}{2}$"

Size of rectangle to cut: 5" × $8\frac{1}{2}$"

1. Cut a rectangle 5" × $8\frac{1}{2}$" (page 32). Divide the unfinished height of the rectangle in half: 5" ÷ 2 = $2\frac{1}{2}$". With the ruler, measure in from the side of the rectangle $2\frac{1}{2}$" and place a small pencil mark on the top and bottom of the rectangle. These marks indicate the middle of the rectangle.

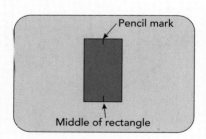

Pencil mark

Middle of rectangle

2. Place the ruler diagonally on the rectangle so the 45° marking lines up with the pencil marks. Cut.

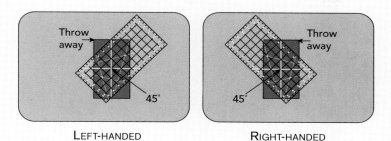

LEFT-HANDED   RIGHT-HANDED

3. Rotate the mat 90° (one quarter turn). Place the ruler so the opposite 45° marking runs through the pencil mark. Cut. Repeat to cut the other end of the rectangle.

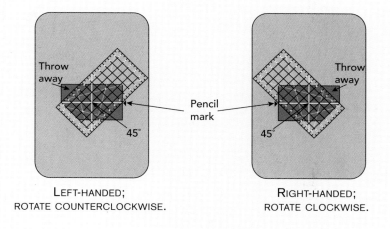

LEFT-HANDED;   RIGHT-HANDED;
ROTATE COUNTERCLOCKWISE.   ROTATE CLOCKWISE.

Cutting a Single Prism

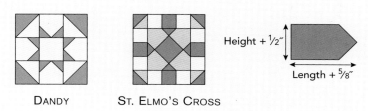

DANDY   ST. ELMO'S CROSS   Height + ½″   Length + ⅝″

Determine the size rectangle needed. Cut one end as above.

Cutting a Hexagon

  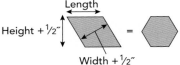

STAR OF   HONEYCOMB
BETHLEHEM

Hexagons are cut by first cutting a 60° diamond. The height and width of a hexagon, measured from flat side to flat side, are the same, just as in a 60° diamond.

Example: Desired finished hexagon height: $4\frac{1}{2}''$

$$4\frac{1}{2}'' + \frac{1}{2}'' = 5''$$

Height of strip to cut: $5''$

1. Cut a strip $5'' \times 40''$ (page 22).

2. Cut a 60° diamond (Steps 2–3, page 40) using the 5″ marking on your ruler. Place the diamond on the mat so the short points are facing the top and bottom of the mat.

3. For this step, you must always divide the unfinished height of the 60° diamond in half. In this example: $5'' \div 2 = 2\frac{1}{2}''$. Place the ruler so that the $2\frac{1}{2}''$ marking runs through the two short points. For added accuracy, check that the upper 60° marking is aligned on one of the lower edges of the diamond as shown. Cut.

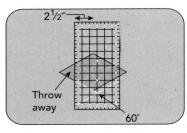 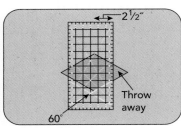

LEFT-HANDED   RIGHT-HANDED

4. Rotate the mat 180° (one half turn). Place the ruler so that the 2½″ marking again runs through the two short points. For added accuracy make sure the upper 60° marking is on the bottom edge of the hexagon. Cut.

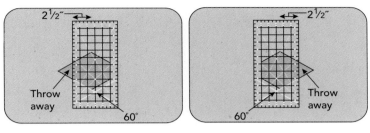

LEFT-HANDED   RIGHT-HANDED

Cutting an Octagon

MODIFIED TRIPLE LINK
SNOWBALL CHAIN

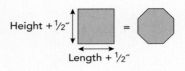

Height + $\frac{1}{2}$″   =

Length + $\frac{1}{2}$″

An octagon is a square with the four corners cut off.

Example: Desired finished octagon size: $4\frac{1}{2}$″

$4\frac{1}{2}$″ + $\frac{1}{2}$″ = 5″

Size of square to cut: 5″

1. Cut a square 5″ × 5″ (page 24).

2. Place the square diagonally on the mat, wrong side up. Draw a diagonal pencil line from corner to corner across the square in both directions.

3. Divide the size of the unfinished square in half. In this example: 5″ ÷ 2 = $2\frac{1}{2}$″. Place the ruler so that the $2\frac{1}{2}$″ marking is on top of the vertical pencil line. Cut.

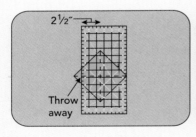

LEFT-HANDED

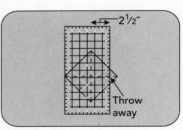

RIGHT-HANDED

4. Rotate the mat 180° (one half turn). Place the ruler so that the 2½″ marking again covers the same vertical pencil lines. Cut.

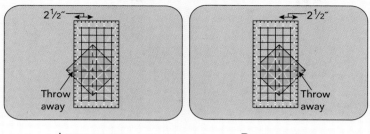

LEFT-HANDED   RIGHT-HANDED

5. Turn the mat 90° (one quarter turn). Place the ruler so that the 2½″ marking is on top of the second vertical pencil line. Cut.

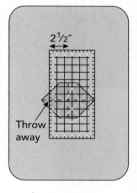 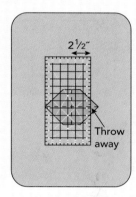

LEFT-HANDED   RIGHT-HANDED

6. Turn the mat 180° (one half turn). Place the ruler so that the 2½″ line again covers the second vertical pencil line. Cut.

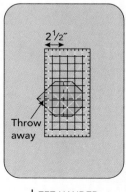 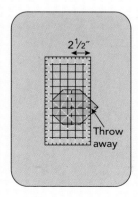

LEFT-HANDED   RIGHT-HANDED

Cutting a Kite

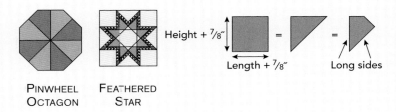

Height + ⁷⁄₈˝   Length + ⁷⁄₈˝   Long sides

PINWHEEL   FEATHERED
OCTAGON   STAR

The two short sides of the kite must be equal in length. The two long sides must also be equal in length.

Example: Desired finished length of one long side: 4⅛˝

4⅛˝ + ⁷⁄₈˝ = 5˝

Size of square to cut: 5˝ × 5˝

1. Cut a square 5˝ × 5˝ (page 24); then cut the square in half diagonally once to make half-square triangles (page 26).

2. Position one of the triangles so that the long bias edge faces the top of the mat.

3. Align the top of the ruler with the top of the triangle, with the tip of the triangle at the 5˝ marking (unfinished size of the square). Cut.

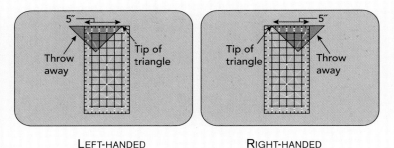

LEFT-HANDED   RIGHT-HANDED

Squaring Up a Block

Despite your careful attention when cutting, sewing, and pressing, your quilt blocks will sometimes be slightly out of square. To square up miniature blocks, I usually use a 6″ square (with the 3″ grid) ruler. For larger blocks, I use either the 9½″, 12½″, or 15″ square ruler. For really big blocks, I use the 20½″ square Omnigrip ruler.

I will show you two methods of squaring up a 12½″ unfinished LeMoyne Star block using the same square ruler. Either method may be used to square up virtually any block.

METHOD 1

1. Divide the unfinished block size (12½″) in half: 12½″ ÷ 2 = 6¼″. Locate the 6¼″ marking on the top and on the right edge of a 15″ square Omnigrid ruler. Notice that the 6¼″ marking from the top intersects with the 6¼″ marking from the right edge.

2. Place the 6¼″ intersection point at the center of the 12½″ star block. Trim any excess fabric that's beyond the top and right edges of the ruler.

3. Rotate the mat 180° (one half turn). Repeat Step 2.

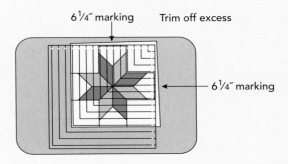

6¼″ marking   Trim off excess

6¼″ marking

METHOD 2

1. Turn the ruler so that you see yellow lines that run horizontally along the top (bottom of ruler), turn the corner, and run vertically down the right edge of the ruler. These solid yellow lines are spaced every ¼".

2. Place the ruler on top of the 12½" block so that the star points on the top and right side of the block are touching the first ¼" yellow line. Remember that the bottom of the ruler will be at the top of the block. Trim any excess fabric that's beyond the top and· right edges of the ruler.

3. Rotate the mat 180° (one half turn) and repeat Step 2. You now have a perfect ¼" seam allowance around the whole block.

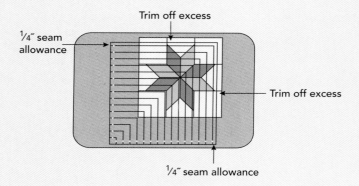

Trim off excess

¼" seam allowance

Trim off excess

¼" seam allowance

> **NOTE** Be very careful when trimming. Always be sure you leave a ¼" seam allowance around the whole block.

Omnigrid Scissors

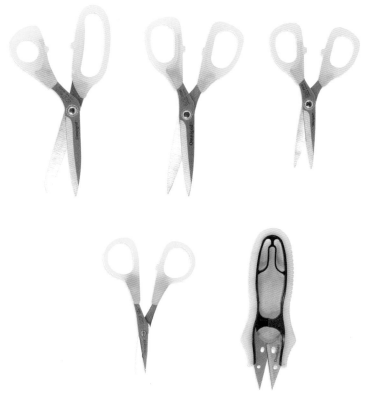

8½″, 6½″, AND 5½″ FABRIC SCISSORS;
NEEDLECRAFT SCISSORS; AND THREAD SNIPS

There will be times when you just can't rotary cut the shape you need; for example, you might need to fussy-cut a flower motif. Omnigrid scissors will let you successfully cut around any shape. They feature a soft handle with precision blades and points. I had to re-learn how to cut with scissors once I started using them. Why? Because they are so sharp right to the point! I can make cuts as short as ⅛″ using just the point of the scissors. I love 'em!

28mm Omnigrid Rotary Cutter

28MM OMNIGRID ROTARY CUTTER AND BLADES

The 28mm rotary cutter has the same features as the 45mm cutter except that the handle and blade are proportionally smaller in size. You'll find that this cutter is perfect for cutting around acrylic templates.

Glow-Line Tape

GLOW-LINE TAPE

Place Glow-Line transparent tape on the bottom of your ruler to highlight measurements used repeatedly during a project. It will save you time and reduce eyestrain when you need to find the same measurement over and over. Simply peel off the tape when you're done. It will not leave any residue.

Invisigrip

INVISIGRIP

Apply Invisigrip clear vinyl cling to the back of your Omnigrid rulers for non-slip rotary cutting. The ruler will not move about once you apply pressure on it. Invisigrip can be easily removed without leaving any residue on your ruler.

This non-slip vinyl is a must for the backs of templates. The template won't slip while you trace or cut around it.

After applying Invisigrip to the back of your rulers, cut any leftovers into narrow strips and wrap them around spools of thread to hold loose ends.

Problem Solving Guide

PROBLEM	PREVENTION	SOLUTION
Rotary Cutter		
Hand fatigues while cutting.	Refer to pages 6–10 for tips on selecting and handling your cutter.	Cut with the bottom of the cutter in the palm of your hand, and place your first finger on the etched ridge on the side of the cutter.
	Don't allow lint to built up around the blade, preventing it from moving freely.	Clean the cutter frequently and put a small drop of sewing machine oil on the blade when you assemble it.
	The blade may be dull; install a new blade frequently.	Replace dull blade.
Rotary cutter skips threads.	Keep a sharp blade in the cutter. Examine cutter blade for nicks if you drop it. Do not cut over pins.	Blade has been nicked and must be replaced.
Rotary cutter drags through fabric.	Maintain proper blade tension.	Loosen or tighten the screw as appropriate.
	Always keep a sharp blade in your cutter. Change the blade regularly.	Change the blade. It may be dull.
	Develop a feel for using uniform hand pressure on the cutter.	Apply more pressure.
	Don't try to cut too many layers of fabric.	Same as Prevention.
	Always hold the cutter at a 45° angle to the ruler.	Increase or decrease the angle to 45°.
Blades dull quickly.	Do not cut on wood, glass, or plastic.	Purchase a mat designed for rotary cutting.
Cut strips are not straight; there is a slight V at the fold.	Always re-square the fabric with the fold every 6″ (page 20).	Don't try to use strips that are not absolutely straight. Cut new strips.
	Do not move the fabric from right to left during cutting. Rotate the mat 180° (one half turn) instead and then continue cutting.	Develop a habit of rotating the mat instead of rotating the fabric on the mat.

PROBLEM	PREVENTION	SOLUTION
Ruler		
Pattern requires shapes with a dimension ending in $\frac{1}{8}''$, for example, a $2\frac{1}{8}''$ square.	Buy a ruler that has $\frac{1}{8}''$ markings, such as an Omnigrid or Omnigrip ruler.	Do not try to guess where the $\frac{1}{8}''$ line would be. Purchase the right ruler.
Cannot see markings on ruler when working with dark fabric.	Buy a ruler with contrasting color values. This is a must for accurate cutting.	Same as Prevention.
Printing on ruler seems inaccurate.	Purchase an Omnigrid or Omnigrip ruler, or compare your present ruler with one made by Omnigrid.	There is no way to fix a ruler that has been inaccurately printed. Buy a new ruler.
Ruler needs to be cleaned.	Treat your ruler with care. Don't put tape, ink markings, and so on on the ruler.	To remove glue, tape, and so on from the ruler, clean it with rubbing alcohol. DO NOT USE nail polish remover.
Ruler doesn't have markings for left-handed person.	Be a wise shopper. Don't buy a ruler that isn't designed for you.	Same as Prevention.
Ruler slips while you cut.	Use the hand walking method (page 21).	Same as Prevention.
	Apply more pressure on the ruler.	Same as Prevention.
	Apply Invisigrip to the bottom of the ruler (page 59).	Same as Prevention.

PROBLEM	PREVENTION	SOLUTION
Cutting Mat		
Dark fabric is hard to see on dark mat.	Buy an Omnigrid mat. It is gray on one side and green on the other.	Same as Prevention.
Cutting mat doesn't lie flat.	DO NOT leave the cutting mat in direct sunlight.	The mat cannot be fixed.
	DO NOT store the cutting mat rolled up. Store the mat flat.	The mat cannot be fixed.
Grids on mat don't line up with ruler markings.	Purchase an Omnigrid or Omnigrip ruler along with an Omnigrid mat.	You cannot fix an inaccurately printed mat or ruler.
Mat has an odor.	Buy an Omnigrid mat and you won't have to worry about an odor.	On some mats the odor will sometimes fade away after use.
Deep cutting lines appear on mat after using wave or pinking blade.	You cannot prevent this from happening.	If you have a reversible mat, use one side for regular rotary cutting and the other side for specialty cutting.
Mat needs to be cleaned.	Don't abuse your mat. Be careful not to get pencil marks, ink, and so on on it.	To clean an Omnigrid mat, rub lightly with a small amount of liquid cleanser or diluted dishwashing liquid. Test on other types of mats first. For very stubborn stains, use a small amount of Comet cleanser.

For more information, ask for a free catalog:
C&T Publishing
P.O. Box 1456
Lafayette, CA 94549
(800) 284-1114
email: ctinfo@ctpub.com
website: www.ctpub.com

For quilting supplies:
Cotton Patch
1025 Brown Ave.
Lafayette, CA 94549
(800) 835-4418 or
(925) 283-7883
email: CottonPa@aol.com
website: www.quiltusa.com

ABOUT THE AUTHOR

Grandma Garrison was Nancy's mentor while she made her first quilt in 1972. Gram told her to cut a 6″ square template from paper and pin it on some fabric. Using regular scissors, quite dull, Nancy cut around the paper template. After cutting about two dozen squares, she noticed some of the squares were not the same size. Nancy called Gram and said, "My blocks don't seem to be the same size." Gram replied, "Are you cutting any of the paper template off when you cut around it? Nancy answered, "No, only once in a while!" That was Nancy's first lesson in accuracy, and it has stuck with her all these years. Today her hallmark is accuracy, and she stresses it with students at every opportunity.

Nancy has written many best-selling books, including *Featherweight 221—The Perfect Portable* and *Rotary Magic*. She also refined techniques for working with squares and rectangles in her other best-selling books, *Block Magic*, *Block Magic, Too!*, *Stars by Magic*, and *Big Block Quilts by Magic*.

Nancy has been a spokesperson for Omnigrid, a division of Prym Consumer USA, Inc., for over sixteen years.

She lives in Pennsylvania with her husband, Frank. They have three grown children. She loves to read mystery novels and work in her flower gardens. To learn more about Nancy, visit her website at www.nancyjohnsonsrebro.com.

Other books by Nancy Johnson-Srebro

Great Titles
from  C&T PUBLISHING

All-in-One
Quilter's
Reference Tool

Easy-to-Follow Charts, Tables & Illustrations

- Yardage Requirements
- Cutting Instructions
- Setting Secrets
- Choosing Supplies
- Piecing Techniques
- Number Conversions & More!

Harriet Hargrave
Sharyn Craig
Alex Anderson
Liz Aneloski

3-in-1 NEW & IMPROVED
COLOR TOOL

NEW & IMPROVED
3-in-1
COLOR TOOL

NOW INCLUDES THESE MUST-HAVE TOOLS!

- Numbered Swatches
- Two Value Finders Green and Red

PLUS

- Color Guide
- Fabric Preview Windows

IDEAL FOR:
Quilting
Crafts
Home décor
Knitting
Sewing
Scrapbooking
Floral design
Graphic design!

JOEN WOLFROM

QUICK & EASY
BLOCK TOOL

QUICK & EASY
BLOCK TOOL

- 102 Rotary-Cut Quilt Blocks in 5 Sizes
- Simple Cutting Charts
- Helpful Reference Tables

IT'S THE QUILTER'S
BEST FRIEND!

- Over 100 block options
- Math-free block charts
- Block index
- Mix 'n match blocks
- Handy pocket guide

Piecing
Tips & Tricks
TOOL

- Piece Like the Experts
- Easy-To-Use Color-Coded Sections
- Everything You Need to Know!

from the EXPERTS:
alex anderson
sharyn craig
carol doak
nancy johnson-srebro
ruth b. mcdowell

Ladies' Art Company
BLOCK TOOL

Ladies' Art Company
BLOCK TOOL

- 160+ Rotary-Cut Blocks
- Rediscovered Gems — Cherished Favorites
- From America's First Mail-Order Pattern Company

A Treasure Trove of
Vintage Blocks!

- 160+ authentic blocks
- Simple no-math yardage charts
- Every block in 5 sizes
- Easy mix 'n match
- Take-anywhere pocket size

Hand & Machine Quilting
Tips & Tricks
TOOL

- Quilt Like the Experts
- Easy-To-Use Quick Reference Guide
- From Planning to Perfect Stitching

Harriet Hargrave
Alex Anderson